Helping Children See Jesus

ISBN: 978-1-64104-051-8

Condemnation
New Testament Volume 19: Romans Part 1

Author: Marilyn Habecker
Illustrator: Frances H. Hertzler
Colorization courtesy of Good Life Ministries
Typesetting and Layout: Morgan Melton, Patricia Pope

© 2018 Bible Visuals International
PO Box 153, Akron, PA 17501-0153
Phone: (717) 859-1131
www.biblevisuals.org

All rights reserved. No part of this publication may be reproduced, stored in a retrieval system or transmitted in any form by any means, electronic, mechanical, photocopy, recording or otherwise, without the prior permission of the publisher, except as provided by USA copyright law.

RELATED ITEMS

To access related items (such as activities, memory verse posters and translated texts) please visit our web store at shop.biblevisuals.org and enter 1019 in the search box on the page.

FREE TEXT DOWNLOAD

To access a FREE printable copy of the teaching text (PDF format) in English or other available languages, enter S1019DL in the search box. Add the item to your cart, and use coupon code XTACSV17 at checkout. Once your order is processed you will receive an email with a link to the free download.

CONDEMN means to:
- declare guilty
- prove guilty
- sentence to punishment

At the conclusion of a trial, an earthly judge (as pictured here) may have to say to a criminal: "You are condemned." The man had been declared guilty, proved guilty and is therefore sentenced to punishment.

Just so, God, the righteous One, judges the world. And He says to those who have not trusted in His Son: "You are condemned."

He that believeth on Him [the Lord Jesus Christ] is not condemned: but he that beleiveth not is condemned already, because he hath not believed in the name of the only begotten Son of God. John 3:18

Lesson 1
WHO ARE CONDEMNED

NOTE TO THE TEACHER

In this Visualized Bible series, there are five volumes on the book of Romans:

Volume 19–Condemnation (Romans 1:18–3:20)
Volume 20–Justification (Romans 3:21–5:11)
Volume 21–Sanctification (Romans 5:12–8:39)
Volume 22–God and Israel (Romans 9:1–11:36)
Volume 23–The Christian's Walk (Romans 12:1–15:33)

Romans is actually a letter written by Paul to the Christians in Rome. He was looking forward to his first visit to that city. Paul may have written from the city of Corinth on his third missionary journey. It is a letter written to believers in Christ, not unbelievers, to help them understand that God is righteous and just.

Our first series is on the subject of condemnation. It is not a pleasant subject but must be understood in order to appreciate God's gift of salvation. Paul shows in the Roman letter that man is absolutely guilty before God and therefore deserves His wrath and punishment. Paul also tells of God's mercy, which brings people to salvation. (See Titus 3:5.) Remember to keep this balance in your own teaching. As you present the wrath of God, present also His love. As you teach about His judgment, teach also of His mercy.

Although you may have taught the conversion of Paul, you should repeat this teaching now. This will help your students to understand that the human author of the book of Romans knew from experience the meaning of *condemnation*.

Scripture to be studied: Romans 1:1-32; Acts 9:1-19

The *aim* of the lesson: To show that Paul knew from experience the meaning of condemnation.

What your students should *know*: God condemns those who reject His Son, but pardons those who receive Him.

What your students should *feel*: An eagerness to have their sins forgiven.

What your students should *do*: Believe in the Lord Jesus Christ and receive Him as Saviour.

Lesson outline (for the teacher's and students' notebooks):

1. Stephen unjustly condemned for faith in Christ (Acts 6:8–7:60).
2. Saul condemned for not believing in Christ (Acts 9:1-6).
3. Saul no longer condemned (Acts 9:6-21).
4. Paul writes God's message of condemnation.

The verse to be memorized:

He that believeth on Him [the Lord Jesus Christ] is not condemned: but he that believeth not is condemned already, because he hath not believed in the name of the only begotten Son of God. (John 3:18)

THE LESSON

Today we begin a study of the book of Romans. Please write in your notebook under the heading ROMANS the theme of the book: "The Righteousness of God" (or "God Is Always Right").

We shall see that God is right in *condemning* sinners. He is right in *justifying* and *sanctifying* believers. He is right in *choosing Israel*.

Does some of this sound like a foreign language? "Condemn," "justify," "sanctify" and "choose" appear often in the Bible. By the time we finish studying Romans, you should understand the meanings of these words and be able to explain them to others. Listen carefully!

Our memory verse contains the word *condemned*. This is the subject of the lessons in this first series on Romans. If we understand the meaning of condemned, we shall understand these lessons. In your notebook, under the title "CONDEMNED," write Romans 1:18–3:20 and the meanings of "condemned" which follow.

First, "condemn" means *to declare guilty*. John came inside and saw some delicious bananas. (*Teacher:* Use a name and a fruit that your students know.) Handing John one banana, his mother said, "You may have only one. I want to take the others to some sick friends." John went outside and ate the banana.

The next time he went inside, Mother was gone. He stuffed two of the biggest bananas under his shirt (or whatever boys wear in your part of the world). He was outdoors again when Mother called: "John, come here! You took some bananas." The bananas were gone and Mother *declared* John *guilty*.

Second, "condemn" also means *to prove guilty*. Mother had not seen John take the bananas, but she saw the bulge in his shirt. "What do you have under your shirt, John?" she asked, lifting his shirt. And right then John was *proved guilty*.

Third, "condemn" means *to sentence to punishment*. "John," Mother said, "we are having your favorite kind of rice (name whatever food your pupils like best) for supper. But because you disobeyed me you cannot have any." So John was *sentenced to punishment*.

What does this have to do with our verse? God has *declared* mankind guilty. "All have sinned," He says. God has *proved* mankind guilty. Even we humans can see the wrong things others do and understand that all are guilty of sin. And God sees much more than we do, for He sees the heart. God has *sentenced to punishment*. He says, "The wages of sin is death." The death He speaks of is that which separates a person from God forever and forever. It is eternal death.

Now let us look at our verse. "He that believeth on Him [the Lord Jesus Christ] is not condemned: but he that believeth not is condemned already." He is *declared guilty*, *proved guilty* and *sentenced to punishment*. Why? "Because he has not believed in the name of the only begotten Son of God."

Every person is in one of two classes. You are either among those who believe in Jesus or among those who do not believe in Him. Believing in Him means putting your trust in Him–the One who died for your sins. Have you put your trust in Christ? If so, you are not condemned. The Lord Jesus Himself said that.

If you have not believed in Him, you are in the other group: "He that believeth not is condemned already." You do not wait until after death to be condemned. You are condemned now. Why? Because you have lied? Because you have stolen? That is not what it says *here*. What does it say? "He that believeth not is condemned already, because he has not believed in the name of the only begotten Son of God." Lying is sin. Stealing is sin. But the Lord Jesus has already taken the punishment for such sins. If you have rejected God's love by not believing in His Son, you are condemned already.

Today we study about one who was condemned but later on was not condemned. In the lessons to follow we shall learn what he has to say about condemnation.

After the Holy Spirit came to the believers on the Day of Pentecost, they obeyed the command of the Lord Jesus to be His witnesses. Everywhere they went they told the Gospel. And many people received Christ as Saviour. The Jewish religious leaders (the Pharisees and the Sadducees) and the rulers in the government (the Sanhedrin) became angry. They tried to force the believers to stop preaching about Jesus. Did the believers obey? No! They continued with boldness, though some of them were seized and beaten. A few were even murdered.

1. STEPHEN UNJUSTLY CONDEMNED FOR FAITH IN CHRIST
Acts 6:8–7:60

Stephen was one of the brave young believers. He preached the Gospel fearlessly. "How can we stop this man?" the Jewish rulers asked each other. "We have to make him keep quiet."

Finally they had an idea. They arranged for Stephen to be tried in court. Then they brought in false witnesses who lied, saying Stephen had spoken against God.

Stephen answered his accusers boldly. At the end of his speech he declared, "You are the ones who murdered the Lord Jesus Christ!"

This made the Jewish rulers furious. But Stephen gazed toward Heaven exclaiming, "Look! The heavens are open. And the Son of Man is standing at God's right hand!"

At this they clapped their hands over their ears and condemned him to death. Dragging him outside the city gates, they hurled heavy stones at him. Bruised and bleeding, Stephen prayed, "Lord Jesus, receive my spirit. Forgive these men for this sin." And he died.

Show Illustration #1

Standing nearby, watching and approving, was Saul. He was probably thinking, *Good! There is one more Christian out of the way. He will never tell anyone else about that Jesus!*

Saul hated the Christians. He broke into their homes and dragged them to prison. He persecuted them so severely that many fled to other provinces. There they obeyed the command of the Lord Jesus and became His witnesses. So the Gospel spread farther.

2. SAUL CONDEMNED FOR NOT BELIEVING IN CHRIST
Acts 9:1-6

Saul was determined to destroy the Christians and their message. When some believers escaped to the Syrian city of Damascus, Saul went after them, determined to see them condemned to death. Near the city a light flashed from Heaven.

Show Illustration #2

Saul shielded his eyes from the brilliant light–brighter than the sun at noon. A voice called from Heaven, "Saul, Saul, why are you persecuting Me?" Saul answered, "Who are You, Lord?"

The voice replied, "I am Jesus whom you are persecuting." Looking up, Saul saw the risen Lord. (See 1 Corinthians 9:1; 15:5-8; Acts 9:17, 27.)

He trembled, remembering the shameful things he had done to Christians. Saul, who once condemned believers to death, was condemned himself–because he had not believed in the Lord Jesus. Remembering his sinfulness and understanding that Jesus truly is the Son of God, Saul asked, "Lord, what do You want me to do?"

3. SAUL NO LONGER CONDEMNED
Acts 9:6-21

The Lord said, "Go to Damascus and wait for further instructions." Saul rose but discovered he had been blinded. So his traveling companions led him to the city. There for three days, without eating or drinking, he waited and prayed.

In another part of the city lived Ananias, a faithful believer. The Lord spoke to Ananias in a dream, telling him to go to the house where Saul was staying. At first Ananias was afraid, for he had heard of Saul's cruelty to the Christians. But the Lord commanded, "Go, for I have chosen this man to speak of Me to Gentiles and kings and Jews."

Show Illustration #3

Ananias went to the house and, laying his hands upon Saul, said, "Brother Saul, the Lord Jesus has sent me so that you may recover your sight and be filled with the Holy Spirit."

Immediately Saul could see again. He got to his feet and was baptized, so all could observe that he now belonged to the Lord Jesus Christ.

Immediately he began to preach the Gospel of the Lord Jesus. This man, who once sent Christians to their death for believing in Christ Jesus, now boldly proclaimed, "Jesus is the Son of God!" Saul's life was completely changed.

4. PAUL WRITES GOD'S MESSAGE OF CONDEMNATION

Saul knew the meaning of condemnation. He had condemned many to death. When he saw the risen Lord, he recognized that he himself was condemned because he had not trusted in the Son of God. But his condemnation was far worse than mere physical death. He would be forever separated from God. All of that was immediately changed on the Damascus Road, however, when Saul believed in Jesus and received Him as Lord and Saviour.

Show Illustration #4

During one of his missionary journeys (now using his Greek name, Paul), he wrote about condemnation in a letter to Christians at Rome. In our next lessons, we shall learn what he said in that letter–for we have a copy of it right here.

Before we look at that letter, I want to ask you an important question. Have you, like Saul, experienced the forgiveness of your sins? Have you put your trust in the Lord Jesus? If you have not, then you are already condemned. You are declared guilty, proved guilty and sentenced to this punishment: eternal separation from God. But God sent His Son, not to condemn the world, but that the world through Him might be saved. (Read John 3:17-18.) Jesus has already taken the punishment for your sins. You may receive forgiveness by believing in Him and receiving Him. Will you do so right now?

Lesson 2
GOD CONDEMNS THE HEATHEN

Scripture to be studied: Romans 1:1-32; Genesis 19:1-25; Jonah 1:1-2; 3:2-10; Ephesians 2:4-7; 2 Peter 3:9

The *aim* of the lesson: To show that when people learn of God's judgment and repent, they escape condemnation.

What your students should *know*: God yearns for everyone to repent. Because He is righteous, He must judge and condemn all who refuse His Son.

What your students should *feel*: Conscious that their sin condemns them.

What your students should *do*:
Unsaved: Repent by turning to God from sin, believing in the Lord Jesus.
Saved: Tell someone this week about God's forgiveness.

Lesson outline (for the teacher's and students' notebooks):
1. God condemns the wicked (Genesis 19:1-25).
2. Nineveh warned of God's judgment (Jonah 1:1-2; 3:2-4).
3. Nineveh repents and turns to God (Jonah 3:5-10).
4. God condemns all who continue in sin, but forgives any who turn to Him (John 3:17-21; Ephesians 2:4-7; 2 Peter 3:9).

The verse to be memorized:

He that believeth on Him [the Lord Jesus Christ] is not condemned: but he that believeth not is condemned already, because he hath not believed in the name of the only begotten Son of God. (John 3:18)

NOTE TO THE TEACHER

In studying Jonah, it is good to give attention to the Ninevites. They sincerely repented when they learned of God's judgment and escaped condemnation. This is in contrast with the Sodomites who did not repent and suffered God's condemnation.

In Romans 9:29 Paul refers to Sodom. So word of that sinful city had doubtless reached Rome. About 20 years after Romans was written, the city of Pompeii (also in Italy) was destroyed by the eruption of the volcano, Mt. Vesuvius. Pompeii was such a wicked city that, before its destruction, someone had written on one of its walls, "Sodoma Gomorra." Even today all that remains of the once beautiful Sodom (and its sister city, Gomorrah) is a reputation for vileness. What a pity! (See Isaiah 1:9-10; 3:9; Jeremiah 23:14; Lamentations 4:6; Amos 4:11; Zephaniah 2:9; Matthew 10:15; 2 Peter 2:6; Jude 7.)

REVIEW

1. What Bible book did we begin studying in our last lesson? (*Romans*)
2. Who wrote Romans? (*Paul*)
3. Where was he when he wrote to the Romans? (*Probably in Corinth*)
4. What is the theme of Romans? (*The Righteousness of God or God Is Always Right*)
5. Our memory verse includes the subject we are now studying. What is it? (*Condemnation*)
6. What does "condemn" mean? (*To declare guilty; to prove guilty; to sentence to punishment*)
7. Before Saul became a Christian, to what did he condemned many believers? (*Physical death*)
8. Is God's condemnation physical death? (*It may include that, but it is much more.*)
9. After life is over what happens to those whom God condemns? (*They are separated from God forever and ever.*)
10. Why are people condemned by God? (*Because they have not believed in His Son, the Lord Jesus Christ.*)

THE LESSON

The Apostle Paul, called Saul in our previous lesson, was an energetic missionary. He went to many cities in various countries to preach the Gospel. Paul was also a teaching missionary. After leaving new believers established in a church, he wrote letters to them, adding to the teaching he had already given them. Paul had never visited Rome. But he was so eager to teach the believers in Rome, that he wrote them even before he got there. (See Romans 1:10-11.) It is that letter–the Epistle to the Romans–which we are studying in this series.

Although Paul was the human writer of the letter, it was the Holy Spirit who guided his writing. Just as Paul's sermons were messages from God, so the letters he wrote are the messages of God. What he preached and wrote are as much for us today as they were for those to whom Paul addressed them. Many lives have been changed as a result of reading Romans. It is important that we carefully study these lessons about that book.

Because Paul was a citizen of Rome, he was acquainted with the Roman Forum. Forums were usually located in the marketplaces or public squares. There the people discussed questions of interest. If a criminal had to go on trial, he was tried at the forum. Paul must have been thinking of that practice when he wrote his letter. He wanted the Roman believers always to remember that the true and living God is righteous and just. In His rightness, God sits over the forum of the world and judges every person.

In this letter God mentions, first of all, people who have not heard the Gospel (Romans 1:18-32). Because God made everyone, He knows what is inside each heart. He says that all people know in their hearts that there is a God (verse 19). They can see things He made. The earth about them and the sky above them prove how great and powerful He is. So they have no excuse for saying they do not know there is a God (verse 20).

They know about Him, God says. But they are not thankful to Him for all the good things He does for them. Instead of honoring Him–the perfect, holy God–they carve images of men and birds, beasts, serpents and creeping things, and call these their gods. Instead of worshiping the living God who created all things, they worship the things He created (verses 21-23, 25).

God lets them do all the vile things they want to and they become worse and worse. They know–for their conscience tells them so–that God will destroy them for doing these wicked things. Yet they go right on doing them–and try to get others to do them!

1. GOD CONDEMNS THE WICKED
Genesis 19:1-25

Because God is righteous and just, He has the right to judge all people everywhere. And He says they are guilty. Because they are proved guilty, they are sentenced to everlasting separation from Him. They are condemned.

Perhaps you are thinking, *Will the God who loves really condemn people whom He has created? He would never do a thing like that!*

Indeed, He has done this very thing!

Hundreds of years before Paul wrote to the Romans, the far-away city of Sodom was known for its wickedness. Sodom and the area around it were so beautiful that they were like "the garden of the Lord." (See Genesis 13:10.) The people of Sodom never gave thought to the God who had made the beauty around them. Instead of loving God, they became the vilest of sinners. Their evil reputation was known even in the distant city of Rome.

In the entire city of Sodom there was only one man, Lot, who loved and worshiped the Lord God. Angel messengers came from God and warned Lot saying, "Get your family and take them out of here. The Lord has sent us to destroy this city." God had condemned Sodom.

Lot hesitated so the angels took him. his wife and two daughters by the hand and led them outside the city. "Escape for your life!" the angels commanded. "Don't look back. Hurry!"

Show Illustration #5

When Lot and his family were safely away, God sent a fierce, unusual storm. The sky opened and hot melted stone and fire rained down from Heaven destroying everything–all the people, every growing thing, the city and the entire area around it. It was too late for anyone to repent of sin. God's condemnation had come. So complete was the ruin of Sodom that even today not a trace of that once fertile plain can be found. Nothing lives or moves there, not even the wind! God turned the great city of Sodom into a heap of ashes, so everyone would know the awful consequences of sin.

Does God always treat people this way–without warning them to turn to Him? No, not always. He knows everything and He knows those who will turn to Him. So He sends His messengers to warn such people.

2. NINEVEH WARNED OF GOD'S JUDGMENT
Jonah 1:1-2; 3:2-4

About 1,000 years after Sodom was destroyed, there was another wicked city, Nineveh. It was larger than any other city of its day. It was so big that it took three days to walk through all its streets. Nineveh was surrounded by a wall so wide that three chariots (wagons pulled by horses) could travel side by side on top of the wall. It was great in size. It was also great in wickedness.

Nineveh's sins rose up before God like smoke travels upward from a fire. The people had turned against the Lord and were living in wickedness: lying, cheating, stealing, killing. God had to condemn this wickedness. So He told His servant, Jonah, "Arise, go to Nineveh, that great city and preach what I tell you."

Show Illustration #6

Jonah went through the gates. Up one street and down another he shouted, "There are only 40 days until Nineveh will be destroyed!"

God never takes pleasure in punishing those whom He has created. And because He is not willing that any should perish, He sent Jonah to warn the Ninevites of His condemnation of their sin.

3. NINEVEH REPENTS AND TURNS TO GOD
Jonah 3:5-10

The people of Nineveh listened to Jonah and believed what he said. They saw their sinfulness as God must have seen it, and they knew they deserved His condemnation. They were ashamed of their wrongdoing. Each one, from the oldest to the youngest, and from the greatest to the least, repented of his sins.

Show Illustration #7

Even the king repented. Stepping down from his royal throne, he took off his kingly robes. Dressing himself in rough cloth, he sat down in ashes to show that he was truly repentant for his evil deeds. He sent this command to the entire city: "Let no one, not even the animals, eat or drink. Let everyone cry mightily to God. All must turn from their evil ways."

And God, who sees all things and understands the thoughts of each heart, saw that the people of Nineveh were truly sorry for their sin and repented. They had turned to Him and away from their evil ways. They cried to God and He answered their prayers. Instead of destroying the city of Nineveh, God forgave their sins and removed their condemnation.

What had the people of Sodom and Nineveh done to deserve God's condemnation? They had been guilty of the very sins about which the Apostle Paul warned the Romans. They had refused to recognize and worship God as the one true and living God. He has shown by His creation how glorious He is. But instead of believing in Him, they turned to idols. They thought of themselves as being all-wise, when really they were foolish and without understanding. Because they refused God, He gave them over to their own uncleanness. They dishonored their bodies. Their minds were filled with wickedness. They were proud, disobedient, hateful. They practiced every evil thing. Sodom continued in its wickedness. But Nineveh turned to God.

4. GOD CONDEMNS ALL WHO CONTINUE IN SIN, BUT FORGIVES ANY WHO TURN TO HIM
John 3:17-21; Ephesians 2:4-7; 2 Peter 3:9

God's Word tells us many things about ourselves. He sees all things and He knows the wickedness that is in each human heart. In His sight each unbeliever is as sinful as the people of Sodom and Nineveh–and the heathen of whom Paul wrote. Each of us deserves God's condemnation. What is His condemnation?

Show Illustration #8

God's Son, the Lord Jesus, is the light of the world. But men have chosen their own darkness instead of His light because their deeds are evil. Those who do wrong hate the light and keep away from it, for fear their sin will be seen. So, because they willfully choose their sins, they are condemned by God. But those who believe in the Lord Jesus, and turn to Him, are forgiven of their sin. They are not condemned.

What about you? Are you condemned or not condemned? If you are not condemned, what about your family? Your neighbors? Your friends? Have they heard that without Christ they are condemned? Have they heard from you that God waits to forgive their sin and remove their condemnation? Will you tell them this week? Today?

Lesson 3
GOD CONDEMNS GENTILES AND JEWS

Scripture to be studied: Romans 2:1-29; Exodus 1:14-17; 19:1-25; 32:1-35

The *aim* of the lesson: To show that God expects Jews and Gentiles to worship Him alone and punishes any who disobey.

What your students should *know*: God desires worship and obedience.

What your students should *feel*: Sorrow for sins.

What your students should *do*: Trust in Christ, the Son of God.

Lesson outline (for the teacher's and students' notebooks):

1. Paul, a slave for God (Romans 1:1).
2. God's people, slaves of Egypt (Exodus 1:14-17).
3. The God of miracles (Exodus 14:21-31; 16:1-22; 17:1-7; 13:21-22).
4. God condemns sinners (Exodus 32:1-28).

The verse to be memorized:
> *He that believeth on Him [the Lord Jesus Christ] is not condemned: but he that believeth not is condemned already, because he hath not believed in the name of the only begotten Son of God.* (John 3:18)

NOTE TO THE TEACHER

Study and teach each lesson carefully and prayerfully. Your students must perfectly understand the meaning of condemnation. So it may be necessary to make two or three lessons out of each one.

In all these lessons we see that God is the perfect Judge. He, the righteous One, can say what is right and what is wrong. He is right when He says that every person has done wrong. He has the right to decide on the punishment for wrongdoing. Even when He condemns, He is righteous!

THE LESSON

Saul had once hated the Gospel of Christ. He hunted Christians, captured them and sent them to death. He even took part in the stoning of Stephen. He thought he was doing God a favor.

Show Illustration #9a

Do you remember what happened to Saul on the road to Damascus? (Encourage student discussion.)

1. PAUL, A SLAVE FOR GOD
Romans 1:1

After his conversion Saul was a changed man. Using his Greek name, Paul, he fearlessly preached the good news of salvation. Instead of hating the Lord Jesus, he loved Him devotedly. He gave himself to the Lord, serving Him as a slave serves a master. He did not serve because he had to. Nor did he serve with awful fear. He served because he wanted to. He served happily. In his letter to the Romans, he referred to himself as a slave (1:1). While writing, he doubtless thought of the ceremony which God had ordered hundreds of years before. (See Exodus 21:1-6; Deuteronomy 15:12-17.)

Show Illustration #9b

Some slaves, when they were set free by their masters, refused to leave. Such a slave would say, "I love my master . . . I will not go out free." He stood at the door of his master's home while his master bored a small hole in the lower soft part of his ear. This was a sign to all that he could have gone free. He could have earned a living some other way. But by this act he was saying, "I love my master. Service to my master is so wonderful that I would rather serve him than go out and be free."

Paul spoke of himself as that kind of willing slave. He had once been condemned. Now, because he had placed his trust in the Lord Jesus Christ, he was not condemned. Because of his love for the One who changed his life completely, Paul chose to be His slave forever. He served God by preaching. He served the Lord by writing letters of instruction to Christian believers.

Early in his letter to the Roman Christians, Paul reminded them that God pronounces the whole world guilty. All people everywhere, he said, have around and above them the beautiful things which God has created. Yet they refuse to honor and worship Him. Instead, they make little idols of men and birds and beasts and creeping things, call them their gods and worship them. They refuse to worship the Creator. In turn, they practice all kinds of sinful things.

Each person everywhere has a conscience which God gave him. His conscience tells him when he does wrong. But he pays no attention. He continues in his own sinful way. And God, who is righteous and perfectly just, says such people are condemned. They will be separated from Him forever and ever.

The Roman Christians were surrounded by untaught and uneducated people who needed to hear the Gospel of Jesus Christ. But in that city there were also many who were just the opposite of the poor and untaught. These were well-educated Gentiles. (Gentiles are people who are not Jews.) The Gentiles thought of themselves as being good. They may have agreed that sinful, poor people should be declared guilty and worthy of death. They doubtless thought to themselves, *We do not sin the way they do. We are nice people and have many possessions. This must prove that God is pleased with us.*

Paul writes, "Because God is kind to you, you should turn to Him and repent of your sin of rejecting His Son. God knows your heart. He, the Judge of all the earth, says you are condemned. Why? Because you have refused His love by not trusting in His Son."

2. GOD'S PEOPLE, SLAVES OF EGYPT
Exodus 1:14-17

There were yet others in the city of Rome along with the high- and low-class Gentiles. These were the religious Jews. Jews are a favored people. Of all the people in the world, God chose them in a special way for Himself. Why He did so is not told. But God is righteous and He always does right. He is perfectly just. Because He is the Creator of all, He can choose whom He wishes. He has the right to do so.

To His special people, the Jews, God gave commandments. And Paul, the messenger of God, writes that the Jews who were proud of receiving the Law, were guilty of breaking that Law. Like the Gentiles, the Jews were condemned by God. Would God punish His chosen people? He would, and He did!

– 23 –

Hundreds of years before Paul wrote his letter to the Romans, the Jews had been out of their homeland for a long time. They were foreigners in the land of Egypt. And the Egyptians used them as slaves.

These Egyptian slave masters treated the Jews cruelly, making their lives miserable. They forced them to work in their fields and in their homes. They compelled the Jews to build cities, often treating them like animals. The Egyptians required them to mix clay and straw, and bake the building bricks. When the Jews cried out against their harsh treatment, the king said, "Since you have time to complain, you must not have enough to do. From now on you must gather your own straw for the bricks. That will keep you busy. But you must make exactly as many bricks as before!"

Of course the Jews could not make as many bricks when they also had to gather the straw.

Show Illustration #10

So they were beaten by the heartless Egyptian slave masters. Oh, how they suffered! If only God would hear their cries and deliver them out of their slavery!

3. THE GOD OF MIRACLES
Exodus 14:21-31; 16:1-22; 17:1-7; 13:21-22

God *did* hear their cries. He always hears the prayers of His children. And He promised to lead them out of Egypt into their own land. There they would be free.

God chose for them a good leader, Moses. To get the Jews (there were many thousands of them) out of Egypt and through the wilderness to their homeland, took many miracles. But the true and living God of Heaven is the God of miracles.

Show Illustration #11a

Once God opened a dry path through the middle of a sea so the Jews could cross safely to the other side. The Egyptians raced to recapture them. But God caused the waters to come together again. And the Egyptians were drowned. (See Exodus 14:21-31.)

Show Illustration #11b

At another time the Jewish people were hungry. So God rained food down from Heaven. It was manna–a kind of food His people had never eaten before. They could have plenty to eat, simply by picking it up. (See Exodus 16:1-22.)

Show Illustration #11c

When the people were thirsty, God miraculously made water flow from a rock. And they had more than enough to drink. (See Exodus 17:1-7.)

Show Illustration #11d

There were no paths through the wilderness. But God guided them. In the daytime He led them by a great cloud. At night the cloud became a pillar of fire which glowed brightly in the darkness. The cloud and the fire reminded the people that God was with them. (See Exodus 13:21-22.)

How tenderly God cared for His people, the Jews! Do you think they loved and obeyed Him? Do you think these people who knew what it meant to be slaves in Egypt became love-slaves of the Lord God? They promised Moses, their leader, "All that the Lord says, we shall do." (See Exodus 19:8.) But did they?

4. GOD CONDEMNS SINNERS
Exodus 32:1-28

One day God called Moses up onto a mountain. The Jewish people were to wait below, while God gave Moses certain laws which they were to follow. Days passed and Moses did not return, for God had many things to tell him. The people grew restless, asking, "Where is Moses? When is he coming down from the mountain? Has something happened to him?"

Forgetting how many wonderful miracles God had done for them, they said to Aaron (Moses' brother), "Make us gods that will go before us. As for Moses, we do not know what has become of him."

Show Illustration #12

Aaron led them in making an idol– the image of a calf. Then the people had a great feast. They sang and danced and bowed down to worship their idol. "This is the god which brought us out of Egypt," they said. After all the miracles God did for them, they turned their backs on Him. They rejected His love and worshiped an image they had made with their own hands.

The true and living God of Heaven saw what His people were doing. Because He is holy, He cannot, will not, approve sin. And He condemns sinners. So that very day God declared His people guilty. His punishment came swiftly, for that night 3,000 men lay dead!

Do you think it pleased God to punish His people? No! Because He is the God of love, He never wants to punish anyone. However, in addition to being loving, God is righteous and just. He knows that ever since the first man and woman (Adam and Eve) sinned, everyone has come into this world as a sinner. As a result, each one sins.

And sin must be punished. God punished the heathen city of Sodom because of its sin. God punished His people, the Jews, because of their sin. And *your* sin must be punished. But here is good news! Your sin has already been punished. For when the Lord Jesus died on the cross, He who never sinned took all your sin–and the sin of the whole world–upon Himself. By putting your trust in Christ, God will forgive your sin. And He, the righteous One, will place you in right standing with Himself. (See Romans 3:9-31.) For whoever puts his trust in God's Son is not condemned. But whoever does not put his trust in Him is condemned already. Will you trust Him right now?

Lesson 4
CONDEMNATION

Scripture to be studied: Romans 1:18–3:20; Psalm 14:1-3

The *aim* of the lesson: To make clear from God's Word, the following truths:
1. God's love does not prevent His condemning sinners to eternal punishment.
2. We have positively no goodness within ourselves.
3. We can do absolutely nothing of ourselves to escape God's judgment.

What your students should *know*: God desires each individual to repent and escape the punishment for sin.

What your students should *feel*: A keen desire to believe in the Lord Jesus Christ.

What your unsaved students should *do*: Accept Christ as Saviour.

Lesson outline (for the teacher's and students' notebooks):
1. God's love and wrath (John 3:18-21, 36; Romans 1:18).
2. Condemnation explained (John 3:18, 36; Romans 3:23; 6:23).
3. Conscience and creation reveal God (Romans 1:19-20).
4. Future judgment for all (Matthew 25:31-46; Revelation 20:11-15).

The verse to be memorized:

He that believeth on Him [the Lord Jesus Christ] is not condemned: but he that believeth not is condemned already, because he hath not believed in the name of the only begotten Son of God. (John 3:18)

NOTE TO THE TEACHER

It is important to remember that God's character is in perfect balance. His mercy does not exceed His justice. His justice does not overrule His mercy. This is difficult for us to understand because of our imperfections.

Carefully study all Scripture references. Begin the lesson by asking the 10 review questions which appear in lesson #2.

THE LESSON

Who will tell a story that shows the meaning of condemnation? (Someone may tell about the boy who took the bananas, as given in lesson #1. If so, fine. After that is told, ask for another illustration–one which may have happened in their own family. Give them time to think.)

Without looking in your notebook, who will tell the meanings of the word "condemn"? (*It means to declare guilty; to prove guilty; to sentence to punishment.*)

1. GOD'S LOVE AND WRATH
John 3:18-21, 36; Romans 1:18

The true and living God of Heaven is the God of love. He loves the world so much that He gave His own precious Son to take the punishment for the sins of all people everywhere. God is patient. He is kind and full of mercy. He gives people opportunity to receive His gift of salvation and repent of their evil ways.

But God is not the God of love only. If He were, He would have to love the evil deeds people do: lying, cheating, stealing, hating, murdering. This is not possible. God is holy and perfect: He can never love sin. Because He is God, He must condemn sin.

Sin is from Satan, the enemy of God, and God cannot and will not approve it. If a person deliberately refuses God's gift of salvation and continues in sin, then God's condemnation is already upon that person. Who will quote John 3:18? "He that believeth on Him [the Lord Jesus Christ] is not condemned: but he that believeth not is condemned already, because he hath not believed in the name of the only begotten Son of God." In that same chapter of John (3:36) is a similar verse which tells us that the person who puts his trust in the Son has life that lasts forever. The one who does not trust in the Son will not have life, but the wrath of God is on him. (*Teacher:* If possible, allow students to read this verse for themselves.)

Show Illustration #13

God who is always right and just, insists that everyone must believe in His Son, the Lord Jesus Christ. His precious blood was the price which He paid for our sins. Anyone who rejects God's love and refuses to trust in His Son, is already condemned. The fire in our illustration speaks of the wrath of God. The darkness is a reminder that men usually rob houses and commit other sins in the night. They love darkness because the things they do are sinful. Sinners who have rejected the Lord Jesus are in the greatest darkness of all. (See John 3:19-21.) And when life is over they will be separated from God in the blackness of darkness forever.

But the light in our illustration reminds us that those who have placed their trust in God's dear Son are not condemned.

2. CONDEMNATION EXPLAINED
John 3:18, 36; Romans 3:23; 6:23

There are four facts you should know about condemnation. Please write them in your notebook. Get them also into your mind and heart.

Show Illustration #14a

1. God's condemnation is NOW.

God showed His mercy in sparing the city of Nineveh when its people turned to Him and repented of their sin. He removed their condemnation. (In our illustration, the light to the right of the cross reminds us of condemnation removed.)

But God condemned the Jews who, instead of worshiping Him, worshiped the golden calf. He also condemned the sinful city of Sodom, destroying it and making it an example of His punishment for wickedness. (The darkness to the left of the cross reminds us of His condemnation.)

Right now God's wrath is upon those who have not believed in His Son. (See John 3:18, 36.) At this very moment they are condemned. When life is over they will be forever separated from God.

Show Illustration #14b

2. God's condemnation INCLUDES ALL.

God sees that people everywhere *do* sinful things and *think* sinful thoughts. They sin because they are sinners. God says, "All have sinned."

Show Illustration #14c

3. God's condemnation is CERTAIN.

Sometimes a person thinks he can hide his sin. His neighbors and even his family may not know about it. But he can't hide from God. God sees and knows every sin. God demands that sin must be punished. There is no escape. If that person deliberately refuses to trust in the Lord Jesus, then one day he himself will have to accept the punishment for his sin. And that punishment is separation from God forever.

Show Illustration #14d

4. God's condemnation is JUST (or right).

God says that sin must be punished. But God is not unfair. He, the One who is always right and always does right, did something marvelous. He sent His only Son into the world and caused Him, the perfect One, to take upon Himself all our sin. (See Isaiah 53:6; 1 Peter 2:24.) Because the Lord Jesus loves us He gave His precious blood on the cross for us. The punishment for our sin has already been placed upon the Son of God. God has done everything He can for us. He is just.

Never forget it. God's condemnation is *now*, it *includes all*, it is *certain*, and His condemnation is *just*.

3. CONSCIENCE AND CREATION REVEAL GOD
Romans 1:19-20

But what about those who do not know God? Will they be condemned for their wrongdoing? Yes, they will. This question is answered in the first three chapters of Romans. Paul writes there the message of God, saying, "All are without excuse" (Romans 1:19-20). "There is none that doeth good, no not one" (Romans 3:12).

Show Illustration #15

God created each of us with a conscience–something inside us which tells us right from wrong. A man who did not know God described his conscience as a three-cornered piece of metal in his heart. When he did wrong, he said, the metal turned and made a little groove which hurt. But finally he had done so many wrong things that the groove was deep and the corners of the metal were worn down. So now, when he sinned, it hardly hurt at all.

In addition to our conscience which speaks to us of our sins, we also have God's creation–the things He made–which tell us about Him. Have you ever watched a bird or smelled the lovely fragrance of a flower and wondered how it came to be? Have you ever stood outdoors on a clear, starry night and gazed up into the sky? Did you wonder who made the stars, or how they stayed there, away out in space? Did you ever think about all the beautiful colors and wonder who planned them–the fiery red of a sunset, the cool green of the grass, and the clear blue of a cold, deep lake? All these amazing wonders prove there is a God in Heaven who made them all. They could never have simply *happened*. When we feel heat, we know that there must be a fire; when we see light, we know that it has a source; if we smell a sweet fragrance, we know that something is causing it. So it is with the things around and above us. Someone had to plan and create them. And that Someone is the eternal, all-powerful, righteous God.

In some places of the world, people have never been taught of the one true and living God. But there is something inside them that causes them to want to worship. They may mistakenly worship the sun, or the moon, or animals, or idols, because they do not understand *whom* to worship or *how* to worship. Yet they sense that somewhere there is a power greater than themselves who should be honored in some way.

4. FUTURE JUDGMENT FOR ALL
Matthew 25:31-46; Revelation 20:11-15

Show Illustration #16

One day you and I and everyone from every part of the world will stand before God–the One who is righteous and just. And anyone who has deliberately rejected the warning of his own conscience and ignored the evidence of nature will have no excuse. He, the guilty one, will know then that he is condemned. He will have to be punished for his sins.

Those who have heard the truth of the Gospel of Jesus Christ and have refused it, will receive even greater condemnation. When the Lord Jesus spoke of the day when people will stand before Him, He mentioned two cities. He said that the doom of the wicked city of Sodom would be more bearable than the punishment that will come to those who reject Him. (See Matthew 11:20-24.) And, He said, the people of Nineveh would condemn those who refused to repent of their evil deeds. (See Matthew 12:41-42.)

If you have not already done so, will you, this moment, receive God's offer of salvation? Once you believe that the Lord Jesus Christ is the Son of God and put your trust in Him, you are not condemned. This is His Word.

www.ingramcontent.com/pod-product-compliance
Lightning Source LLC
Chambersburg PA
CBHW060803090426
42736CB00002B/138